Eternal garden

by

Bioluminescent Drea

CONTENTS

Prologue

This book is a combination between gardening and the philosophy of life. If we learn to observe Nature, there are a lot of patterns that show us how to find equilibrium not only in our garden but also in our lives.

A Gardener can be considered an artist. While a painter performs their artwork painting on a canvas or some objects, a garden is a gardener's canvas. A gardener paints the world with plants, shrubs, and trees. Whereas a painter uses paints to beautify places or inspire some ideas and evoke some emotions in humans; a gardener uses life to decorate, rejuvenate, regenerate, and detoxify the world as well as giving food sources to insects and herbivores.

While a painting doesn't change (apart from being gradually deteriorated due to light and humidity or other factors), our garden keeps changing; one of the reasons why it is interesting and it reminds us that life is transient. A painter hopes that their artworks won't change or deteriorate, while a gardener embraces or even adores change.

We should never take anything for granted and learn to appreciate the beauty of nature since every flower we see takes a lot of energy and resources from the plant to produce and it will last just for a shorttime.

I would like to express my gratitude to all those who love the planet and try to contribute, in one way or another, to protecting, healing, and detoxifying it. This book is meant to promote regenerative gardening as well as love and respect for Nature. I wish with all my heart for all of you to find equilibrium and inner peace, the true happiness that can be cultivated on Earth and the key to peace and harmony in the world...

Chapter 1: Perennial Garden

I only grow perennials in my garden because they live for a long time and since I hate seeing anything under my care die and I don't like wasting money, time, and energy; annual plants don't agree with my natural tendency, while perennials tick all the boxes. Like all of you, I have many things to do in my life and no matter how much I want to look after my garden constantly, I cannot afford it. Thus, perennials are a much better option than annuals for me.

Perennials improve the soil because their roots are much deeper than annual or biannual, which allows microorganisms to grow around the roots and the more beneficial microorganism in the soil, the better the quality of soil becomes.

When I first started to create my garden, I just focused on evergreen perennials. One of the main reasons why I love evergreen perennials—apart from the fact that they look good all year—is that they capture carbon from the air all year round while deciduous and herbaceous plants can absorb carbon from the air only when they don't shed their leaves.

That said, I have also grown to love herbaceous and deciduous perennials as well, especially perennial bulbs. I adore perennial bulbs for many reasons, but one of the most fascinating things about them is the fact that they lay dormant for some time, then spring back to life to bless me every single year—which gives me a sweet promise and somehow brings me hope.

Every year I can't wait to see their shoots rise out of the darkness beneath the earth, cherish sunlight, and bloom again. Furthermore, bulbs can be used together with shrubs and trees to add more flowers to our garden and make the garden more interesting. I usually grow perennial bulbs around the trees and bushes in my garden and under groundcovers.

I suggest investing your money, time, and energy better by growing more perennials in the garden. A perennial garden is a perfect fit for far-sighted people since it is a kind of investment for a better future. There are a lot of beautiful perennials at least in zone 7. Even when you live in a much hotter or colder zone, you can rest assured that there are always some plants that can survive and thrive in your zone. Nature is tough and will find a way to exist and survive somehow.

When it comes to evergreen perennial trees, I prefer trees and shrubs with a particular color of leaves, trunks, or branches. I am especially fond of variegated leaves like Euonymus, Variegated English Boxwood, variegated dogwood, and Daphne odora 'Aureomaginata'. Their leaves can have different colors other than green, such as blue (Colorado blue spruce, blue cedar, lavender, etc.), red (Sacred bamboo, Japanese pieris, Photinia, and so on), and silver (snow-in-summer, Russian sage, lavender, Helicrysum italicum or curry plant, dusty miller, and so forth). I particularly adore silver-foliage plants since they can also be used in a moon garden; they shine in the moonlight, giving your garden a magical vibe at night.

As for deciduous perennial trees, I prefer the trees with colorful barks because when they shred all their leaves, they still make the garden look beautiful also in the winter. When it comes to the color of the trunks and twigs, my favorite deciduous trees and shrubs are Sango Kaku Japanese Maple (red), dogwood (red or yellow), and birch (white or silver).

One of many positive things about perennials is also related to the fact that perennials will usually grow stronger each year and it is just like taking care of your children and seeing them grow up and make progress in their lives. True love, accompanied by a well-balanced mind, makes you happy no matter who or what you care for or take care of.

Chapter 2: Cultivate Love, Respect, and Gratitude

Just like my life, a garden is not only for me. Although I can't deny that I love plants and flowers, the main reason for me to have a garden is for all others (e.g., bees and pollinators, other types of wildlife, neighbors, and passersby).

Each of us can contribute to our world positively in various ways. One of the many ways I choose to do that is to start my sustainable and regenerative garden. It is my way to express love and respect toward Mother Earth, all living things, as well as all other humans.

My garden brings me immense joy especially when I see wildlife visiting or seeking shelter in my garden and it is equally delightful to see the passersby and neighbors cheered up by its good scent and beauty. The other reason why I have a garden is that taking care of something alive is by far the most joyful, pleasant, and rewarding activity.

Among all living things, plants and trees need so little but give so much more than they take. They need just a bit of humidity, sunlight, and some minerals in the soil, then give back to the environment a hundred times more than they take from it. If that could be considered an example of admirable virtue, I wish I had their virtue and my existence were as benevolent as theirs. Many humans are envious of rich and famous people, but I envy plants since they are true givers and resource generators in our biosphere.

You don't need to have a green thumb to be a good gardener: All you need is love and you will automatically study, learn through trial and error, and become a successful gardener. I started my garden from scratch, and back then I didn't even know how to transfer plants from pots into the soil since I am not a professional or trained gardener, and none of my family members or friends have a passion for plants.

I had never had a garden until then and had killed almost all my house plants. Since I started my garden, my love for plants and trees has helped me to learn and discover a lot of things about gardening. Now all plants (both indoor and outdoor), or almost all, have survived, and many of them even thrive.

Compared with humans, plants are much more forgiving, much more grateful, much less complicated, much less demanding, and incredibly resilient. All parents make mistakes, in one way or another, and our children, as well as the world around them, will pay for our mistakes; which is why most, if not all, parents are stressed. Being a parent to plants, however, is completely stress-free, and taking care of plants will only give us relaxation and bliss.

My deciduous and herbaceous perennials come back to bless all of us every year. My corn plant (Dracaena Fragrans), for example, blooms every year, which is a very rare phenomenon where I live (zone 7a). What's more, for over 15 years this plant has been living with us, I have never given any fertilizer (apart from its dry leaves) and have changed pots only twice using normal garden soil; yet, it looks happy and never fails to give us its sweet-scented flowers every single year.

There is only one thing I usually do when it comes to fertilizer for both my indoor and outdoor plants: I never throw away dry leaves —as long as they are healthy and disease-free—and bury them around their trees. In this way, the trees get their nutrients back and this method is completely sustainable.

Plants are the most grateful sentient beings; when you truly love them and learn how to take care of them, they will overwhelmingly love you back. We constantly depend on Nature to survive and thrive. The only problem is we usually take things for granted. We receive all fundamental things for our survival from nature and Mother Earth, but we ignore them and focus on what we don't have—which makes us live miserably. Nature teaches me about gratitude and true giving, hence inner peace and true happiness.

Plants need both your love and knowledge to survive and thrive, and all you need to do is to study and try by yourself since, like all other fields of knowledge, practicing is fundamental for your success. The key to success is, certainly, knowledge accompanied by love and respect toward Nature.

My garden is completely free from artificial chemical substances because I respect Mother Earth and all living things. Synthetic fertilizers, weedkillers, fungicides, pesticides, and insecticides are harmful to the environment; if we love Mother Earth as well as all living things including ourselves, we will never use them.

Plants and trees do not only give food sources, shelter, and nurseries to wildlife, but they also absorb toxic substances from the environment and neutralize them. They purify and detoxify the environment around them as well as helping people to feel more relaxed and peaceful—there is a body of research about that. Thus, they are good for us both physically, psychologically, and spiritually.

Gardening teaches us simplicity, humbleness, peace, and gratitude. Accordingly, gardening is a synonym for cultivating love and respect toward Mother Nature, Earth, all living things, and ourselves.

Chapter 3: Non-toxic Garden

As I mentioned before, the garden is not supposed to be just for us but for all other humans and living things around us, so I avoid using synthetic chemicals in my garden and have always used natural insecticides and fungicides if need be.

As for a weedkiller, I pour vinegar on weeds, and most of the time, it works very well against all types of weeds even couch grass (Elymus repens), the immortal Evil in my garden. When we bought the house, a couch grass had already got established in the garden, so it was extremely difficult to eradicate.

After many failed attempts, I have finally discovered the easiest, the most effective, and the most inexpensive way to kill couch grasses. Of all the weeds I have found in my garden, Couch grasses are among the toughest to kill since they can spread and cover a lot of space.

Even though the websites usually mentioned that their roots are shallow, the couch grasses in my garden have very deep roots, about 20 inches. Just little pieces of their roots are left in the soil, and in no time, the whole lawn will be covered by them again. Shallow-rooted plants for me are those benevolent groundcovers that occupy only a surface of the ground, protecting the soil from weeds.

Greedy weeds are usually deep-rooted and hard to kill while beneficial plants tend to be more fragile and sensitive. When we use synthetic chemicals to kill weeds or bad insects, they also kill good guys. While harmful and greedy (micro)organisms usually spring back to life in a very short time, beneficial and positive ones take much more time to recover and come back; which is why we should try to avoid using artificial chemicals at all costs.

I have learned some effective formulae against fundal disease such as the mixture of baking soda, and organic dish soap. While garlic mixed with hot chili is good against bad insects. However, I am not an expert when it comes to natural fungicides and insecticides, so you should seek advice from the experts.

In any case, whatever natural remedy you choose, please make sure that you do not harm bees or beneficial insects. You also need to keep in mind that if you provide good soil and the plants are healthy, bad insects or diseases will hardly attack them. What's more, if you provide all food sources for beneficial animals and insects, they will keep taking care of your garden and you will need to work much less.

Chapter 4: The Importance of Soil

Soil is fundamental for the health of plants. Healthy soil is beneficial for plants to grow. According to Dr. Elaine Ingham, a soil biologist, contrary to what most people believe (including me before listening to her), all the mineral nutrients plants need are already in the soil, but they need to be converted to soluble forms for plants to be able to use them.

Without beneficial microorganisms, all mineral nutrients will remain locked up in the soil. Soil is already rich in minerals but it needs these microorganisms to digest them and release them in an edible form of nutrients for plants and trees to use them.

Therefore, all we need is to add life and not minerals to the soil. Adding minerals to the soil might even be negative to the plants. For example, when we add potassium to the soil, it will bind with magnesium, and the plants cannot get magnesium from the soil. Hence, animals and humans who eat those plants will not get magnesium from them.

The best strategy is to allow Nature to work for you because she sees all the interconnection and co-relation in a food web. We don't usually see the interconnectedness and chemistry as she does, and our lack of knowledge will make us choose the solution that might hurt us or just solve one problem but cause many other problems.

The problem of unhealthy soil is not a lack of nutrients but that of lives or beneficial organisms: benevolent fungi, bacteria, nematodes, and protozoa. We need to add compost to the soil in our gardens not because the soil lacks nutrients but because we need these microorganisms to break down the compounds of the minerals already existent in the soil and make them available for the plants to absorb them.

Since life is of the utmost importance for the health of the soil, weedkillers and any hostile artificial substances are harmful to the soil. These harmful chemicals do not only kill bad guys but also annihilate all good guys. We have evolved from the same ancestors and in one way or another we are interconnected; it is very hard to find something harmful to some life forms and completely harmless to others.

This is the main reason why insecticides, fungicides, and weedkillers are not safe—no matter how much big chemical companies try to convince us to sell their products to make them richer.

The wisest way is to add beneficial microorganisms into the soil to help it find equilibrium and become positive for plants and trees and not to add toxins into the soil and the environment. What's more, many artificial substances remain in the environment for a long time, so they also cause toxic accumulation in the environment.

Compost is fundamental for all benevolent microorganisms in the soil. However, some acidophilic plants, such as camelias, rhododendrons, azalea, and dogwoods need some more help. I usually slice orange peels or pineapple peels and core, chop them into tiny pieces, then put them around the roots of these acidophilic plants since they will naturally and gradually raise the soil pH. It is a win-win situation since I love eating citrus fruits and pineapple and instead of throwing their peels away, I can use them for my garden.

The rule of thumb is to let the soil undisturbed as much as possible and perennials are a perfect choice also for this reason.

While you will have to disturb the soil every year if you grow annuals, perennials just need to be left alone and thrive by themselves, spreading more and more roots—which is positive for all microorganisms in the soil. Please don't forget that the soil is a house of microorganisms. Imagine some giant comes to destroy your house every year or twice a year. I bet you wouldn't be happy about that either.

Chapter 5: Alternative Lawn

I opt for an alternative lawn for the sake of bees and other pollinators. I choose creeping thymes instead of classical grass for many reasons. To begin with, they are low-growing (maximum height without flowers: 1-2 inches); hence, we don't need to mow the lawn and it helps us save both time and energy. In addition, once established, they hardly need water; in this way, we also save water. Furthermore, they grow well in poor soil, so we don't need to add fertilizers.

They also bloom profusely for 2 months or more and give food sources to pollinators. When they are in bloom, the plants are completely covered with bees. What's more, they are evergreen (at least in zone 7) and resist both extreme heat and cold very well.

They even give off a wonderful scent when you step on them. Yes, you can walk on them just like a classical grass lawn. Interestingly, they also create an extremely dense carpet of leaves, so they effectively choke out weeds; at the same time, they are kind to what grows underneath, which makes them perfect for bulb planting.

Additionally, they are low-maintenance. Once established, they take care of themselves and spread forever. Sometimes, my neighbors' cats pee or poop on them, and the part of the plant at that spot usually dies out; all I need to do is to remove that damaged spot and the plant will regrow and form a dense mat again. Last but not least, it is believed that they are mosquito repellant although I cannot guarantee that this is true. All in all, they are completely environmentally friendly.

I have grown three cultivars of ground-hugging thymes (i.e., Thymus serpyllum 'Red Carpet', woolly thyme, and Thymus citriodorus 'Doone Valley') because they bloom at different times; this way, bees will have a food supply for a much longer time. In my garden woolly thymes bloom first, then Red Carpet, and then Doone Valley.

This year, 2022, the driest and hottest year in Italy and many parts of the world, the creeping thymes have proved to be the most resistant of all. Even weeds have died out while creeping thymes survive without water at all.

Even though creeping thymes might not thrive in your hardiness zone, there are a lot of choices of ground-hugging plants that look beautiful and environmentally friendly. I don't choose a classical grass lawn since it needs a lot of time, energy, and all resources; it is not sustainable and absolutely not environmentally friendly. This planet is to be shared by all living things, so as Homo sapiens sapiens (or wise man in Latin), it is our direct responsibility and duty to try to heal the planet we have poisoned and give the world back to wildlife.

Chapter 6: Year-round Interest

A good garden must look beautiful all year round, which is why I grow all bulbs and perennial trees. Evergreen perennials provide beautiful and fresh background for your garden, but you don't need to plant just evergreen since many deciduous trees and shrubs can decorate your garden with beautiful and colorful trunks and branches also in the winter.

I prefer to grow trees and bushes that have different colors of leaves because I love to add as much color as possible to my garden. I am also obsessed with variegated leaves and flowers because they look much more interesting than plain ones.

If we choose plants correctly, we will have flowers in our garden throughout the entire year. Winter-blooming plants are not easy to find, but in my garden Clematis cirrhosa var. *purpurascens* 'Freckles', 'Landowne Gem', and 'Advent Bells' bloom in winter usually from November to February, whereas Hellebores also bloom happily in the snow.

We can build layer upon layer of flowers too. For example, together with perennial plants, we can grow many layers of spring, summer, and bulbs. The best autumn bulb, so far, is Colchicum 'Waterlily', which will grow even in poor and shallow soil.

It is not enough to have all types of perennials that cover your garden in each season. For example, if you have spring-blooming plants, you should find something that can bloom at different times in spring: early, mid, and late and the same method should also be applied to summer, autumn, and winter-blooming bulbs.

You should find plants and trees that bloom not just in spring or autumn or winter but also bloom at different times in their blooming seasons. Ideally, it would be best to find free flowering plants that can cover even 2 seasons or repeat blooming. If you look hard enough, you will find that many plants bloom in two seasons, spring and autumn.

A beautiful all-year-round garden is like how we live our lives. We can live well at all ages. Spring represents the time when we are born and young, summer when we are young adults, autumn when we reach middle age, and winter when we become old. When we love and respect others and always try to give to the world as much as we can and much more than we take, our lives are beautiful at any age. If I were to be born again, that is the only way I would choose to live. Let's make our garden of life beautiful in all seasons.

If I were to choose my two favorite seasons though, I would pick spring and autumn. Everybody loves spring and I couldn't agree more, but autumn also has its unique beauty. In any case, all seasons are beautiful if we learn to appreciate and benefit from them.

Nothing is more exciting than spring. It is full of promises and hope. My spring-blooming perennial bulbs give me immense joy when their shoot start appearing above ground. When trees start to wake up and remind me that they are still alive, it fills my heart with happiness.

Spring is a synonym for Paradise on Earth to me. People generally appreciate spring flowers and I love them too, but what really excites me is when I see the tiny green shoots from plants, the very first sign of life. Although I have never been a biological mother to anyone, I can completely understand what's it like to have my heart filled with joy and hope when we see the beginning of life.

The world is decorated with flowers in spring. Early spring, in particular, is the most special period of the season to me, especially when I see my bulbs sprouting out of the ground and the trees starting to wake up and all signs of life are beginning to emerge. This always fills my heart with joy and sweet promises.

Autumn, however, is not less joyful than spring. In Fall, the world is adorned with colorful leaves, and the color the Fall decorates the world is even on a larger scale. The autumn leaf color is so warm that it always makes me feel relaxed and calm. Autumn is like humans in their middle age—in my opinion, one of the most beautiful periods of our lives since we have learned to embrace our pain much better and relate our pain to that of others.

At this age, we become more tolerant and tend to forgive more because we have experienced both joy and suffering, which allows us to see the big picture of life. In any case, we can make our lives as well as our garden beautiful in all seasons. There are always plants and bulbs for each season and there are always positive things we can do in all stages of life.

The same plant grown in different angles of your garden can bloom at different times. My creeping thymes, for example, bloom earlier in full sun and much later in part shade; which is perfect for bees and other pollinators since it means that they will also have access to food sources for a much longer time.

Summer is the season when lilies, daylilies, tiger flowers or Tigridia pavonia, allium, coreopsis, hydrangea, roses, irises, and gladioli in my garden bloom. Undoubtedly, summer is one of the most colorful seasons although I prefer much cooler temperatures and what I dislike the most about summer is mosquitoes, but life has both sides—pleasure and pain.

Winter is not without charm. It is the time when we can see naked tree trunks and branches, which is why I prefer colorful tree trunks like Coral Bark Maple and dogwood. There are many trees with beautiful and colorful trunks that I don't/can't have, such as Rainbow Eucalyptus (Eucalyptus deglupta), Chinese Red Birch (Betula albosinensis), Tibetan Cherry (Prunus serrula), Chinese Parasol Tree (Firmiana simplex), Paper Birch (Betula papyrifera), Japanese Stewartia (Stewartia pseudocamellia), and Paperback Maple (Acer griseum).

Although flowers are rarer in winter in zone 7, some plants even bloom happily in snow, a winter-blooming Hellebore is one of them. When it comes to flowers, nothing can beat the tropical rainforest zone, but I don't live in that climate zone, so I will have to create my own paradise using cold-hardy species. There are plants and flowers for all types of climates in the world. However, if we live where nature is quite harsh, we can also create microclimates, but also need to find a way to make them as sustainable as possible.

Winter symbolizes our old age and it is not easy for anyone. However, those who live benevolently reap the benefit also at their old age. Some of them even have a productive, (almost) painless, and blissful life also at that stage of life. Hence, in my book, they represent a remarkably beautiful winter garden.

If we live our lives guided by love for all and not for just a few groups of people/things; we will never feel lonely, bitter, dissatisfied, or depressed in our old age. I am lucky enough to have seen both examples: those who live their lives benevolently and are kind to all and those who live egocentrically and inflict pain on others.

The former live happily also when they are old and die in peace, while the latter live unhappily when they are old—or rather, in almost all stages of life—and die in agony. Indeed, I have never seen anyone more frightened of death than they are.

Ironically, the former should fear death because they are happy with themselves, their lives, and those around them; whereas the latter are unhappy with themselves and others, yet they are so scared of death.

The former should fear death because they have a wonderful life and they need to leave all people and things they love behind, while the latter should be more than happy to be gone because their existence causes them as well as those around them so much pain. Nevertheless, those who live benevolently and are positive for those around them always go in peace.

Those who harm others never end well and they inevitably have a painful old age. All dictators, narcissists, perpetrators, or abusers always face tragic ends; all you need to do is look at their life stories and you will clearly see why I have made this assumption.

Universal or All-encompassing Love guarantees our happiness in our old age. Although we stop working, we will find something useful and positive to do and somehow provide services to the world even at that age. Even though all of us make mistakes, if we learn to love universally and not selectively or limitedly, we will find our way back and walk the benevolent path again.

Love and try to give as much as you can in any stage of your life, and you will become a beautiful garden all year round. Even at the end of your life, you will leave beauty and inspiration behind. In this way, you bless the world both when you are alive and pass away.

Chapter 7: Evergreen Groundcovers

As I mentioned in the chapter on the alternative lawns, we can't leave the ground empty; otherwise, bad plants will grow on it, or if the ground remains empty for a long time, the soil will face degradation. Consequently, you can never let the soil uncovered in any part of your garden. The best way to prevent your soil from being infested by weeds is to cover the ground with the plants of your choice.

To me, the best groundcovers must form a dense carpet. It should be evergreen to provide a year-round cover that will constantly shade the soil protecting it from erosion, limiting the germination of weed seeds, and giving shelter to overwintering beneficial insects and pollinators.

In my opinion, one of the best evergreen groundcovers is creeping thyme since it forms a dense blanket on the soil, is low-growing (1 to 2 inches long), produces flowers for 2-3 months, and sometimes it also reblooms in Fall. Indeed, when it blooms, the plant is smothered in small flowers, attracting all pollinators, especially bees. I use this plant as an eco-friendly alternative to a grassy lawn and I have never regretted my decision.

Creeping thymes give off a very nice scent when we step on them and since it is ground-hugging there is no need to mow the lawn. What's more, they resist both extreme heat and cold as well as drought.

However, creeping thymes thrive in full sun and disdain shade.

Thus, you will need to use other low-growing plants that will also thrive in shade: Vinca minor, Lamium, *Brunnera macrophylla* 'Jack Frost', Ajuga reptans 'Black Scallop', creeping Jenny, and so on.

Evergreen groundcovers don't need to be ground-hugging since it depends on your aim and purpose. If you use them as an alternative lawn, you will certainly need something very low-growing, so much so that you don't need to cut it down; while in 'other situations you can opt for something taller.

My favorite groundcovers around the pond, in any case, is Creeping Jenny or Lysimachia nummularia of which I have both cultivars, 'Goldilocks' and 'Aurea'. They are low-growing, spread around the pond, and gracefully trail into the water—softening the edges of the pond and perfectly uniting the dry land and water.

I am especially drawn to low-growing groundcovers simply because I can do so many things with them. I can use it to simply cover the ground and protect it from soil degradation and weeds or I can plant bulbs underneath. Whatever the case, they are all beneficial to my garden.

Chapter 8: Fragrant Garden

A garden is supposed to be universally good or positive to all. Accordingly, it is supposed to look good as well as smell good for all passersby and our neighbors, which is why I fixate on fragrant plants and flowers.

I have both evergreen and deciduous fragrant flowers in my garden: Daphne odora, fragrant roses, jasmine, honeysuckle, peony, sweet-fragrant daffodils such as 'Bridal Crown' (my favorite), hyacinth, lily of the valley, lily (though I must admit I don't particularly like its scent but I grow it for its look), freesia and begonia (they are not hardy in my zone, so I grow it in a pot and put it indoor in winter).

A scent has a stronger impact on us than what we think. Some scents can bring back your childhood memories, some can cheer you up, while others can upset you. I prefer to please others and cheer them up, so I prefer to grow fragrant flowers. There are so many ways to love others and this is one of them, giving them a pleasant smell to lighten up their days.

Chapter 9: Water Garden

It is of the utmost importance to provide a water source in your garden to attract wild animals into your garden as well as giving food and water supply to them. You don't need to have a big space in the garden to have a pond and can use anything resistant enough as a container and bury it underground just to give a chance to wildlife like frogs to have access to the pond. You don't even need to have a garden since you can also create a water garden on the balcony by using any container to build a small water garden.

You need to grow oxygenating plants in your little pond and can introduce into the pond some predators to eat mosquito larvae and pupae, such as Killifishes, topminnows, or any fish that can live outdoors in your climate zone. However, once you have a water pond, nature will also help you because they are many things in nature that eat mosquito larvae, e.g., dragonfly larvae, damselfly nymphs, tadpoles, water striders, and other predators.

The best position of a pond should be in full sun because many sun-loving plants like lotuses and water lilies won't bloom without at least 6 hours of sunlight. You should try to avoid building a pond under a big tree because it will shadow your pond and its fallen leaves into the pond will increase ammonia, nitrite, and nitrate in the water.

Ideally, the pond should have different levels of depth and the deepest part of a pond should be about 60 to 80 centimeters. It shouldn't be deeper than 1-meter for 2 main reasons. First, if it is too deep, it is also not easy to clean. Second, lotuses, as well as many other plants, usually cannot live in water deeper than one meter. Ideally, the pond should have different levels of depth since it will allow you to have different types of aquatic plants.

When the pond is too shallow, however, it can lead to a series of problems. If you have fish, they might not survive winter, and too shallow a water in full sun will call forth algal blooms because the water temperature will be very warm during summer, in which condition algae and cyanobacteria will thrive.

If you have access to rainwater, it is the best option for the water in the pond; if you don't, you will have to make do with tap water, which must be dechlorinated before using it to fill in the pond. Unfortunately, chlorine, like most synthetic chemicals, is not conducive to life. You can use synthetic chemicals can dechlorinate your water, but I prefer the natural approach.

Chlorine is quite simple to eliminate; you will just need to leave the water stay in a container without a lid for 1 day, and chlorine will evaporate by itself. However, many local governors use chloramine instead of chlorine, and it takes 3 times as much to break it down. I can't possibly know whether the governor chooses to use chlorine or chloramine, so to play it safe, I usually leave it in full sun for 3 days—sunlight also helps fasten the evaporation process.

You can add a water aerator into the pond to discourage mosquitoes to lay eggs since they usually prefer still water. A water bubbler is not only good as a prohibitor of mosquitoes, but it also adds oxygen to water, from which aquatic animals can benefit.

Unlike, an aquarium, the pond doesn't need water changing, which is positive for the environment since it also means you will save lots of water. All you need to do is to let the water get all the beneficial bacteria and find equilibrium. You need snails and shrimps or a clean-up crew or detritivores together with diatoms and beneficial bacteria in your pond to keep the water clean.

Like all other living things, aquatic animals need equilibrium to survive and thrive, and we need to imitate their natural habitats as much as we can. I don't have any filter and provide just a water fountain to add more oxygen to water, but the most important thing to help purify water is aquatic plants, especially oxygenating plants, and aquatic snails such as Japanese trapdoor (Viviparus malleattus).

Unfortunately, I don't find this species of snail in Italy but I have found the great pond snail (*Lymnaea stagnalis), which is one of the best choices since this species is endemic because it has more chance of survival in an outdoor pond.* Ideally, any type of snail that can survive winter outdoors will do. The best option, however, should be the endemic species of where you live. In this way, it will not disrupt the balance in the ecosystem as we don't introduce the species that haven't evolved in the place.

However, there might be some negative sides to this type of snail. While the great pond snail can eat live plants when they don't have enough food, some types of snails such as Japanese trapdoor and the great ramshorn (Planorbarius corneus), according to the aficionados of freshwater snails, will never eat live plants but only dead ones. The great ramshorn can also be used as an indication of the purity of water since it will die out if the water is not pure.

If you have tadpoles and dragonfly or damselfly nymphs in your pond, however, I don't think that you will need fish. Nevertheless, it depends on the size of your pond. If it is big enough to allow species diversity and gives all of them a lot of space, shelter, and food; you can have them all.

I am not an expert when it comes to a water garden, and this is just my opinion and not a rule of thumb. As my target is to protect wildlife, I prefer to see dragonflies, damselflies, and frogs in my garden. That said, eventually, I couldn't resist adding some goldfish into my pond.

Like all other living things, aquatic animals need equilibrium to survive and thrive and we need to imitate their natural habitats as much as we can. Since my main purpose is to make my garden as eco-friendly and sustainable as possible, I keep the use of electricity to a minimum. Hence, I provide just one small pump with a filter with a fountain head to add more oxygen to water as well as purifying it.

I try to add as many plants as possible to help purify water, especially oxygenating plants. I have all types of aquatic plants in my pond: floating such as Floating Fern (Salvinia natans) and European frog-bit (Hydrocharis morsus-ranae); marginal, e.g., Louisiana Iris, Yellow Flag Iris (Iris pseudocorus 'Variegata'), and the Flowering Rush (Butomus umbellatus); submerged, i.e., Floating Heart (Nymphoides peltate), water lily 'Angeligue', Valisneria torta, and Sagittaria subulata; and oxygenating, namely Ceratophyllum Demersum and Elodea densa. The best plant pots for aquatic plants should be full of holes to allow all the roots to come out and absorb all the nutrients in the water and purify it.

My favorite plants are Yellow Flag Irises (Iris pseudocorus) because they are endemic and they have very long roots which filter and purify water efficiently, and the fact that they are also evergreen is the icing on the cake.

The plants around the ponds are also important since they provide shelter to animals and they also look very beautiful. As usual, I prefer perennial plants around the pond, and one of my favorite plants is Creeping Jenny. It covers the ground and some part of it trails inside the water, making it a perfect plant to grow around the pond. I love to add more color to the place around the pond, so Lobelia Fulgens Queen Victoria and Houttuynia Cordata Chameleon are some of my favorite plants around the pond while water irises are my favorite marginal plants but I also grow them around the pond.

Since my water garden is only 5 months old and is absolutely very young, only blue dragonflies occasionally come to visit my garden. Much to my delight, one morning I found the first dragonfly's nymph in my pond and I hope to find many more dragonflies and damselflies in my garden next year.

I have built a pond also for dragonflies and damselflies since wetland ecosystems are being lost to urbanization and unsustainable agricultural practices all around the world and many species of them are endangered. Eighty-seven percent of our wetlands have been lost since 1700. Apart from being useful and beneficial, they are also stunningly beautiful. Although they can bite you if you scare them, their bites are not harmful or poisonous.

Even though we cannot provide them a big natural habitat as they do deserve, if every single one of us provides a small habitat for them, it will give them some more chance to survive. They are one of the most important predators of mosquitoes both in the air and the water.

Since the most annoying mosquitoes in Italy are Asian tiger mosquitoes (Aedes albopictus) which are very active during the day; more dragonflies and damselflies will provide non-toxic, effective, efficient, and inexpensive solutions to our problems.

You don't need to have a big space for a water garden—it is enough to have a small container of water on your balcony and create a small water paradise for aquatic plants and wildlife. You don't even need a water pump if you provide equilibrium to your little pond. Water means life and no living thing can live without it. We are getting rid of water supply and food sources in the wild and now it is high time we did something to save our wildlife by adding water into our garden. It could be just a small container with water on our balcony. If each of us does just a little, together we will do a great thing.

Chapter 10: The First Nests

I have always wanted to see birds nesting in my garden, but I don't have many trees because my garden is quite small. In 2020, it was the first time I found a bird's nest in one of my trees. A black bird laid her eggs on the branches of my scholar tree (Styphnolobium japonicum).

Blackbirds have always visited my garden since the very beginning. The female, in particular, isn't afraid of me at all. She always follows me when I go out to take care of my garden. I guess I have gained her trust. I love it when she comes to take a bath from my garden hose. She and her family eat lots of earthworms and some strawberries in my garden, but I don't mind, especially strawberries, because my garden is, first and foremost, dedicated to wildlife.

I do love earthworms (I always call them the first gardeners) since they are precious for soil, one of the most fundamental things in nature, but I can't interfere with a food web and also because I love birds too.

Not only was 2020 the year of the first bird nest in my garden, but it was also the first solitary bee nest year. I placed an insect hotel in my garden 2 years earlier, but none of the insects had come to make a nest in it until the spring of 2020.

The information from the articles I have read is quite contradictory: some say that it should be south-facing while others suggest north-facing. So, I chose to position my insect hotel facing south but it doesn't have direct sunlight since I give it a little shelter from rain and extreme elements, and it seems to work as I have had many bee nests now.

Solitary bees are important pollinators because while honey bees won't come out from their hives in bad weather, solitary bees do not mind it and pollinate flowers normally. Therefore, solitary bees will fill in where honey bees are missing, which is why biodiversity is fundamental for the survival of the biosphere. When I saw the first solitary bee nest in my insect hotel, I was elated. When one comes, others will follow. Animals talk to each other. Accordingly, against all bad news, 2020 is the year of the first nests.

In the garden, as well as in life, there are always two sides of a coin and we shouldn't just focus on the dark sides of life; in nature, there are both sides. Just the same way that springs come after winter, light comes after darkness. I have never been afraid of the darkness because in the dark I always see light. After extreme cold comes warmth and after death of one life form arise other life forms.

Nature recycles everything, and life is beautiful also because it constantly changes. Death is nothing but a transformation. The most important thing for high consciousness creatures is to make our existence as benevolent as possible so that our lives become a chance to bless the world around us. Living in that way, when our transformation arrives, we will leave our human form without regrets.

Chapter 11: The First Gardeners

As mentioned in chapter 3, we need all beneficial microorganisms to make our soil healthy and rich in nutrients for our plants and trees. These microorganisms are undoubtedly the first and one of the most important gardeners provided to us by Mother Nature. However, there are other organisms worth mentioning and should also be considered as the first gardeners.

My garden is full of earthworms because there is plenty of food for them such as dry leaves. I never throw away dry and fallen leaves as well as some useful weeds (e.g., clover, dandelion, borage) and buried them underground. I don't like leaving them on the ground since I prefer to have a tidy garden and thanks to all shallow-rooted groundcovers, i.e., sedum, creeping thymes, and Peace In The Home (Soleirolia soleirolii), my garden looks tidy enough, but at the same time is full of food source even underground.

I prefer shallow-rooted groundcovers because I can just lift them up without causing any damage and bury all dry leaves and good weeds in the ground underneath them. A good groundcover will knit the uppermost surface soil together and make it look like a dense carpet. I just cut one side of a carpet, dig a deeper hole underneath, put all dry leaves and sometimes very small twigs into the hole, add some more soil, then cover it up with the groundcovers.

My garden is so full of earthworms that it attracts many blackbirds. Although they seem to be insignificant and humble animals, earthworms play the most important role in improving soil quality in our garden. Earthworms increase soil aeration, infiltration, structure, nutrient cycling, water movement, and plant growth. They add oxygen and nitrogen to the soil, helping beneficial bacteria to grow. Their beneficial existence, thus, gives them a title, the first gardeners.

Chapter 12: The Supreme Gardener

The best gardener is Mother Nature, but we need to understand how she works and imitate her and let her work for us. The most unwise way to farm and garden is to fight against Mother Nature. Trying to control nature is one of the missions impossible humans have been struggling to accomplish since the dawn of human civilization.

We have tried and failed thousands, if not millions, of times, yet we have never given up hope. It might be our instinct to try to contradict and manipulate Nature—after all, we are the most rebellious children of Mother Nature and I can't condemn us for that since I dislike blind faith and obedience myself.

Having said that, I still believe that to go against Mother Nature; we will need a lot of energy, time, effort, and resources, as well as a constantly strong will to obtain only disappointing results, and most importantly, we might wreak havoc on the environment.

We also need to clearly distinguish between being rebellious and being disrespectful. We can disagree with someone but should always be respectful. We don't need to agree with everything Mother Nature proposes to us (i.e., all primordial instincts), but we need to keep in our mind that our reason to rebel must never be guided by egocentrism, greed, and ignorance. If we rebel, we should rebel for the right cause.

To date, she has only given to us all the conditions and things we need to help us survive and continue to exist. Subsequently, unless it is extremely necessary, we should try to learn her functions, cooperate with her, and let her give and love us the way she can.

Our effort to reshape the world the way we like and want it to become by using all synthetic chemicals might seem easy and effective in the beginning, but it will eventually end up wreaking havoc on the environment and our health. Hence, we need to respect, listen to her teachings, and benefit from what we learn from her.

Sustainability is obtainable only when we don't work against Mother Nature and use what is already available in nature and we don't need to invent or change in any way. Thus, the most sustainable method is to use what nature already has to offer.

Chapter 13: Biodiversity

A good garden should provide biodiversity because the more variety of plants and trees there are in the garden, the more types of wildlife will visit it. Each species of pollinators has its favorite food, so the more various food we can provide for them, the more diversity of wildlife we will have in our garden.

Why is biodiversity important? Cavendish bananas, a common cultivar of banana we find in the markets all around the world, for example, can be wiped out by a single blow of one disease. However, if a farmer plants different cultivars, at least some of them will survive the disease since they have different genetic makeups, hence different strengths and weaknesses; not to mention that different cultivars also provide different properties of food that can be very useful for our health.

Consequently, not only should we allow different species to survive, but we must also encourage sub-species to thrive. Our monoculture is absolutely not sustainable and overall negative because it goes against nature and this strategy of farming should not be pursued for the sake of both our health and Nature. Since it throws ecosystems out of balance and the soil becomes depleted and poor, a farmer also needs to spend extra money on chemical fertilizers, which damages the soil and the environment even more.

Monoculture is believed to give us more crop yields, and hence help us earn more money. However, most farmers using this classical method of farming, struggle and do not thrive. This is why our classical way of farming is proved to be not as good as we believe; it wrecks our environment, destroying equilibrium as well as keeping the farmers poor.

In my opinion, permaculture is one of the best options because we have to learn to work with Mother Nature and not against her. Nobody can win or cheat Nature, and if we learn to cooperate with her, she is very generous and provides all the solutions to our problems. All we need is to learn how she works and collaborate with her. If we manage to learn to work with her in synchrony; we will save time, energy, resources, and money. Therefore, both gardening and farming should target biodiversity and both our health and that of the planet.

Chapter 14: The Muse

Birds are the Muse of the world. Their songs and presence cheer me up and brighten up the dark days. Some of them are also incredible dancers, e.g., birds of paradise and bowerbirds. Every time I see the documentary about these birds, they crack me up. They look so weird and funny. Apart from blessing the world with their voice, songs, and dancing; birds also have a fair share of eliminating bad bugs in our gardens.

Various species of birds visit my garden all year round: blackbirds, sparrows, tree pipits, robins, tits, turtle doves, magpies, and jackdaws, while hoopoes (Upupidae) and sometimes white wagtails come to bless my garden only in spring and summer. All of them are irresistibly cute and hoopoes are strikingly beautiful when they fly since they have zebra-striped wings and fly in a particular way. They have an undulating flight, which is like that of a butterfly.

Hoopoes' soft and modest hoots are unique and my heart beats faster with joy every time I hear them hooting because it means that they are nesting somewhere nearby and it fills my heart with joy, love, and hope. Their hoots promise me that they will hatch their eggs, allowing their species to continue to exist and grace our world with their presence.

All birds/muses fluff up their feathers in winter to protect themselves from cold, which makes them look like a ball of feathers, and the only reason why I could make out that they are not just a simple ball but a bird is a beak and a tail attached to it. Some of them are extremely fluffy, so much so that they look like they were going to explode.

Birds make me smile every time I hear their songs, or see them. When you truly love something, it always cheers you up every time you see it. I want my garden to offer more food and shelter to wild birds. I know they will take care of my garden, but it is already joyful just to see them and I would love them even if they were useless. In any case, let the Muses take care of your garden and your mood.

Chapter 15: Regenerative Gardening

I never throw away the leaves and flowers of my plants and get rid of them only when they are afflicted by infectious diseases. I usually chopped the leaves and spent flowers into little pieces and burry them around the roots of their own plants. They are the best natural fertilizers for my plants and trees in the garden.

One of the many reasons why I have chosen perennials is to improve soil qualities. Generally, perennials' roots are much deeper and wider than annuals and we don't need to disturb soil like annuals. Please don't forget that the longer you let Nature take care of herself, the better the quality of soil is.

Our soil all over the world becomes toxic and poor due to our monoculture farming and the use of artificial chemical substances. Poor soil means poor nutritional values of our crops. Our crops now, compared to those in the past, have much poorer nutritional values. We have an urgent need to choose regenerative agriculture over harmful monoculture farming, which, to my dismay, is the main type of farming all over the world nowadays.

We poison our world and ourselves by choosing to use all synthetic substances in our farming and the government doesn't do anything substantial to encourage farmers to switch to regenerative agriculture, which is conducive to life and not against life. As long as we use something harmful to life, the world will only be submerged in toxins.

Regenerative agriculture promotes small farms and gardens, so it also helps increase income and the well-being of an individual instead of promoting a huge and greedy agribusiness. It is based on permaculture, agroecology, agroforestry, restoration ecology, keyline design, and holistic management; all of which disciplines focus on respect toward nature and they also tend to be cost-effective. Surprisingly, what is in harmony with nature is also cost-effective and universally good—not good only for a few groups of greedy people. As Homo sapiens, we are supposed to heal the world, and never ail it.

Chapter 16: Equilibrium and Harmony

Good and bad are human values and most of the time they can also be completely subjective and egocentric, while equilibrium is the value of Mother Nature. Humans who are guided by ego and greed might consider something universally bad to be good, whereas equilibrium is objective and the consequence is the harmonious coexistence of all species in the biosphere.

A good garden must find equilibrium and be full of beneficial insects and animals such as bees, ladybugs, birds, hedgehogs, dragonflies, and praying mantes. If you don't use toxic chemical substances and provide food sources like flowers and water as well as shelters, your garden will attract all these benevolent insects and they will thrive and take care of your garden; you will spend less time and energy fighting against all bad insects that can harm your plants.

Mother Nature is generous and wise and provides for us everything we need to survive and thrive. All we need to do is to understand what and where to look for the best solutions she could give. You can use all-natural methods to make your plants healthy. My garden is full of acid-loving plants, such as azaleas, rhododendrons, camelias, dogwoods, and daffodils.

The most natural way to fertilize them for me is to bury their leaves and orange peels around their roots. Orange peels are one of the best natural ways to increase soil acidity. Certainly, they will not give an immediate result since it takes time for any organic material to be processed by microorganisms and absorbed by plants, but if you constantly add them into the soil, you will always replenish the soil with all the nutrients and the level of acidity the plants need. Don't forget to grind or chop them into small pieces though.

I love citrus fruits and my fridge is always full of them, after I eat them, instead of throwing their peels away, I use them to add nutrients to my garden soil. Although I am a cat person and can't help adoring cats; since I started my garden, I have discovered that cats' poop is one of the worst things in my garden. Apart from its incredibly unpleasant odor, it kills my groundcovers.

Nevertheless, I later found the utility of the cats' mess. I usually bury it underground, out of reach of the roots of my groundcovers, all of which are shallow-rooted. Earthworms, as well as other microorganisms, can eat it and turn it into some nutrients in the soil eventually. All these poop eaters help keep my garden soil rich in nutrition.

I use orange peels to raise soil acidity for my acidophilic plants and cover the ground where cats poop. Cats usually poop at the same place and if you put orange peels at that spot, they will never come back. Since cats don't like the smell of orange peels, I usually chop them into little pieces and sprinkle the ground with them. Orange peels work both as a deterrent to cats' poop and nutrients for the soil, so it's a win-win strategy.

Before I discovered the trick, due to my neighbors' cats—some of them are free-ranged, some are feral, while others are not trained to use a litter tray—my lawn was full of brown spots here and there. Cats usually poop in someone else's garden to mark territory and it's also because they have not been trained to use a litter tray properly by their owners.

Most cat owners don't foresee or recognize this problem, in any case. When we become parents, we tend to see only the beautiful sides of our kids because that is what love usually does. The only problem is when we cannot see the harm our children could do to others or take their harmful behavior lightheartedly.

I completely understand those who love cats because although I love all animals, I am a cat person. I find cats irresistible, but if I were to own one, I would prefer to adopt feral cats and not buy them. The main reason why I won't buy cats and would choose to adopt them is that I don't want to encourage this business to grow as cats contribute to the destruction of wildlife, and feral and free-ranged cats are even more harmful to wildlife than those well-taken care of and live in a loving home. We should keep in our mind that of all the mammals on earth, 96% are livestock and humans, and only 4% are wild animals.

That said, I don't believe that cat owners intend to ruin wildlife or harm their neighbors. My neighbors, for example, are wonderful people and most of them are kind-hearted—or at least, I can see much kindness in them and in those who don't care for nature and the environment at all. They are not heartless but they just love and care for different things. Many people are very kind to their human fellows and their pets but are completely indifferent toward wildlife.

Like all ills in the world, all humans' harmful actions derive from their lack of knowledge. Little do the cat owners know that cats contribute to the extinction of many species of wildlife—at least they don't fully realize or if they do, the survival of wildlife is not near and dear to their hearts.

Unfortunately, due to our progress in technology and our way of living, we become alienated from nature, and more and more humans lose touch with Mother Nature. The proverb 'Out of sight, out of mind' can describe why most humans nowadays are so estranged from Nature.

Certainly, we cannot blame any damage done to our lawn or wildlife on the cats. Undoubtedly, it is their owners' responsibility; when we are parents, no matter what kind of life forms they are, we always need to take care of them.

In case they go outside and will somehow affect the world, we need to properly teach/train them to prevent them from harming others; which is why the most difficult living thing to raise is human since children afflicted by bad parenting can harm those around them as well as themselves and compared with cats and dogs, the damage will be on a much larger scale.

Love can blind us, especially when it is selective. Selective love makes us overlook the dark sides of those we love, and many humans still choose humans or those they love personally over Nature, but we forget that our survival depends on the equilibrium of our ecosystem and that the world we leave behind will belong to our children and grandchildren.

Parenthood comes with duties and responsibilities, and the first and most important duty of Homo sapiens parents is to teach our children to learn to love and respect both themselves and others. If we are not ready to nurture and take care of someone or something, we should never become parents and end up harming them, be it plants, animals, or humans. Life is precious and we should never take it for granted, either ours or that of others.

True love brings about harmony and equilibrium both inside and outside of us. Our plants and trees in the garden need our love and knowledge to thrive. Even something that might appear to be harmful, with love and knowledge we can transform it into something useful and positive like cats' poop in my garden.

Nothing is better than letting Mother Nature take care of herself. The problem is our greed/insatiate desire drives us to destroy natural habitats of wildlife at the speed of light causing Nature to lose her equilibrium. Unfortunately, when nature loses balance, many other problems come along with it, and our classical solutions like synthetic substances only make things worse.

As apex predators and the greediest users of resources, humans should be the fewest in number and let the planet be mainly populated by the resource generators like plants and wildlife. To live in harmony and peace both among ourselves and with other living things on Earth, we should focus much more on the quality of our children rather than their quantity. We cannot have both quality and quantity; otherwise, we will suck our Earth Mother dry.

Chapter 17: Indoor Plants

Most of us live indoors much more than outdoors, but we tend to pay attention mainly to our outdoor gardens. In this day and age, synthetic substances are used everywhere and in everything. We are surrounded by or submerged in toxic chemicals in our house—be it material we use to build a house or furniture or objects we use in the house or the chemicals we use to clean or paint the house. Hence, we are in dire need of something that helps detoxify our indoor environment.

If you are lucky enough to have a sunroom or skylight, you can have lots of plants and can also create a vertical garden or hanging baskets indoors. The most important thing is, as always, you need to choose the right plants for the right place. For example, fruit trees will love direct sunlight and a south-facing sunroom is perfect for them, although you might need to spray water on their leaves because some of them need both heat and humidity.

My cumquat and kaffir lime, for example, need some moisture on their leaves, especially during a very hot dry summer and I usually mist them in the morning. I love citrus trees also because their blooms give off an amazingly fresh and sweet scent. A Meyer lemon is among the most frequent bloomers in the citrus family and although I have never grown it myself, lots of gardeners love it.

Another plant that produces sweetly scented flowers in my house is the corn plant or Dracaena fragrans 'Massangeana', but it should never be exposed to direct sunlight and thrives very well in bright indirect sunlight. It's a night bloomer and my house will be blessed by its sweet fragrance for about one month in its blooming season. Mine blooms only once a year, while on some websites, it is mentioned that it can bloom up to three times a year.

I have never moved my Dracaena outdoors and it has remained in the same place for 7 years now and seems to be happy enough. It thrives on neglect because I have never given it any fertilizer apart from its own leaves cut into small pieces that I bury around its roots and it usually gets water once every two weeks. Considering that it needs so little, the fact that it blooms only once a year is more than enough for me and I always count my blessing.

Considering the number of hours we usually stay in our houses, all of us should also focus on indoor plants to detoxify our indoor environment because toxic substances in the house can harm us more than we expect and if we are constantly exposed to toxins, it is highly likely that one day we will get sick when our body accumulates enough toxin and inflammation. Thus, house plants are not just embellishments but necessity.

Chapter 18: Eternal Flowers

The most beautiful garden must always be decorated with flowers and I love to have a succession of flowers both on the ground and on the wall. My favorite combination for climbers is evergreen and deciduous perennial climbers that bloom at different times of the year. Evergreen Armandii Apple Blossom clematis (blooming from February to April), for example, can be planted close to a climbing rose (blooming from mid-spring to autumn).

On the ground, instead, you can plant many layers of bulbs together with perennial plants that bloom during different periods of the year. If you choose well, you will have flowers in your garden all year round although bulbs cannot produce flowers in winter (at least in zone 7), there are some perennial plants that bloom in this season, such as winter honeysuckle, heathers, winter-blooming hellebores, mahonia, evergreen vibernum, witch hazel, winter-blooming camelia (might need shelters in zone 7 and lower), winter jasmine, winter-blooming clematis, winter-blooming rhododendron, and daphne (to me, it is one of the most fragrant flowers).

However, the real reason why I have designed my garden this way is because of pollinators, especially bees. Before having a garden, I had believed that bees hibernate in winter; surprisingly, the very first year I moved into my house, I found bees in my garden.

They usually come to take the nectar from my winter-blooming clematis, winter-flowering heather (or Erica carnea), and hellebores; which made me completely delighted to see that they can find food sources even at that period of the year.

Most people view daffodils as early to mid-spring bloomers but, in reality, there are also some cultivars that will bloom in winter (e.g., Rijnveld's Early Sensation) and Tamar Double White (flowering from winter through to May). In any case, where there is a will, there is a way. There are flowers to grow in all seasons and all types of climates as plants are one of the toughest things on Earth. All you need to do is find the plants that can thrive in your climate zone.

When it comes to indoor flowers, there are endless ways to fill your house with them. Many bulbs, such as tulip, hyacinth, and daffodils can be tricked to bloom at different times of the year and there are many techniques, but they usually need chilling to trigger them to produce flowers. One of many common techniques is to put them in the fridge and you will see hyacinths and daffodils blooming in winter indoors.

Actually, you can use the same technique to force them to bloom at any time of the year; all you need to do is to chill them first. However, not all daffodils need to be chilled. Paperwhite cultivar, for example, doesn't need to be chilled, so you will need to study to understand whether the bulbs of your choice need to be chilled or not. If you choose the right bulbs, your house will be full of flowers all year round.

Chapter 19: Perennial Vegetables and Fruits

Fruits and vegetables are good for our health. I am a fruit enthusiast and will live happily on fruits and meat. Although I wasn't particularly keen on eating vegetables, I have grown to love them in these years. As usual, I prefer perennial vegetables and fruits such as artichokes, asparagus, kales, broccoli, chives, garlic, sage, thyme, oregano, rosemary, fig, strawberries, blackberries, cherries, apples, pears, apricots, apples, persimmon, plum, and the list goes on.

The benefits of perennial vegetables and fruits, like all perennials, are so many; saving money and time is one of them, certainly. Once established, perennials tend to take care of themselves and become more resistant to pests, diseases, drought, and weeds. Many perennials are also very beautiful and ornamental and help build soil since they don't need to be tilled. I highly recommend you cultivate perennial vegetables instead of annuals to help improve soil and save your energy, time, and money.

Some perennial fruit trees take some time to be able to bear fruits and the same goes for perennial vegetables. Asparagus will start to produce a decent crop after 2 years while a standard size apple tree will bear fruits after 8 years.

I do love tropical fruits such as jackfruit, chempedak, and durian and would be overjoyed to see them grow in my garden, but that is the impossible dream as long as I live in zone 7. At least once in your lifetime, I suggest you try chempedak and jackfruit. If you are a fruit lover, chances are you will like them. I adore chempedak and consider it one of the most delicious fruits in the world. Durian, however, due to its odor, might put someone off. Although in my case, its flavor makes me completely forget its stink.

Since I started my garden, I have found great joy in harvesting fruits and vegetables grown in my garden. The fruits and vegetables in your garden usually taste much better than those you find in the supermarket. The strawberries and tomatoes I buy from the supermarket pale in comparison with those I harvest from my garden. What's more, they are much healthier since I haven't used any synthetic substances and relied only on Mother Nature, while the product from the food industry is full of pesticides, fungicides, weedkiller, and growth hormones.

Chapter 20: Problems Are Part of Life

Having a garden, I also learn that many problems found in my garden are caused by others. I can have good soil, the right conditions for plants, natural fertilizers, beneficial animals and insects, etc.; but I can't control other factors coming from the outside of my garden. We are all interconnected, and my garden is also affected.

If my neighbors' garden is full of weeds, my garden will also be infested by them as the wind or animals will carry their seeds to grow in my soil. No matter how much I try to keep my lawn perfect, my neighbor's cats will pee or poop on it and I will have some brown spots. No matter how much I take good care of my roses, a butterfly will lay eggs and the whole plant will be covered by caterpillars.

Although I don't use any toxic substances, my neighbors might spray some synthetic and dangerous insecticides and they might be carried to my garden by the wind. The underground water might get contaminated by the factories in my neighborhood, and the list goes on.

This is the nature of life. Life is difficult because it is conditioned by all others. Living together with others is always complicated because although you are peaceful and never look for trouble, trouble will look for you. That said, it is inevitable as long as we coexist in the world. Problems are, accordingly, an intrinsic part of our lives.

Some of the problems though are easy to solve by myself, whereas others also need others to come together and try to solve them. The problems of weeds are not difficult to solve since if you have gown good groundcovers, you will have much fewer weeds. Cats' poops can be protected by orange peels.

As for the infestation of caterpillars, I don't get rid of them since you can't love butterflies and kill caterpillars. I just grow many more roses. I don't waste money buying more roses, but propagate them from the plants I already have, so I have many more for free.

Insecticides in the air might be tough but hedges can, up to a point, protect you from toxic surroundings. Hedges can break the wind and protect us from some pollution surrounding us. However, contaminated underground water is a big problem that needs both bottom-up and top-down approaches to solve the problem. The problem of our contaminated and off-balance ecosystem is even much bigger and it needs all of us to come together and do what we can to save our planet.

To live a good life, we must never run away from our problems. Although life is full of problems, it's also full of solutions. The only problem is we need to find a wise solution, and whatever solution we choose, it shouldn't be harmful to others.

Those who are benevolent spend most of their lives solving problems caused by others, but that's how they gain satisfaction with their existence and find purpose in their lives. Accordingly, problems are not as bad and as daunting as many people think. Every day in the garden, you will always find things to do and problems to solve, so gardening always helps you improve your problem-solving skills.

Chapter 21:
Perennial Roots

Perennials help increase soil quality as their roots go much deeper and wider than those of the annuals. They help hold the soil together and protect it from erosion. Salt marsh plants are fundamental for saltmarshes since they hold the ground together and reduce coastal erosion and are the best natural flood defenses.

Saltmarshes are very important for wildlife as they provide food, shelter, and nurseries to many species and have inestimable value both ecologically and economically. Salt marsh plants protect saltmarshes as they hold the soil together and without salt marsh plants, saltmarshes will disappear.

Tree and plant roots stabilize the soil and tie the soil layers and prevent the soil from being washed away as well as improving the soil structure. They help prevent mud/landslides, which are dangerous to life and cause damage economically. Such humble and simple trees can help save lives and money.

Surprisingly, the tree roots will keep holding the soil for up to 2 years after the death of the plants. Hence, perennial plants are fundamental for the environment both above and under the ground.

Chapter 22: The Reason to Live

As long as we love, we find our reason to live. When we truly love something or someone, our lives are full of hope. We will hope to see those we love to thrive and will contribute to their success and happiness. Consequently, we will give to them as much as we can, which will give us our reasons to live.

Apart from my family, friends, students, neighbors, knowledge, Nature, and Mother Earth; I also love my garden, and since I have all the perennial plants—especially, herbaceous and deciduous perennials—they give me hope to see them come back to bloom again next year and the year after that.

As long as you love, you are always motivated to live, and the more people and things you love, the more motivation you have. So, based on my direct and indirect life experiences, I firmly believe that love is the best reason to live. It helps us live positively and guides us to try to make our existence useful and helpful to others.

Life is worth living when we learn to love and give truly and when our existence supports other lives and not just our species but also other life forms. Mother Nature and Earth love universally and their target is equilibrium in the ecosystem so that all life forms can exist together. If we just focus on our species and ignore all others, eventually that selective love and egocentrism will destroy us since our survival depends on the health of the whole biosphere.

When we learn to love and give truly, it is impossible to be depressed, and I think the least demanding creatures to take care of are autotrophs.

Plants and trees, especially, give the most since they are autotrophs and they are the first resource generators in the food chain. When we have an abundance of food givers, we are all blessed. On the contrary, when we have too many heterotrophs, especially apex predators and hungry resource consumers like humans, we are cursed since that will only mean conflicts and wars. When we are heartless and ignore the well-being of other living things in nature, that indifference will eventually destroy us.

If we loved Mother Earth and embraced all her other children in our hearts, we would leave space for them and would never destroy their habitats. Overpopulation, as well as its sequelae, has proved that so far, we have only focused on our species, which is egocentrism on a large scale.

That said, it is not because we are evil by nature; we are just indoctrinated to be estranged from Nature. All we need to do is to rekindle our relationship with nature and learn to love, respect, and coexist in harmony with nature again. Living just for ourselves will never fulfill our spiritual needs, and we will never find inner peace and true happiness if we choose to exist that way.

Chapter 23: Let the Garden Heal You and Keep You Healthy

Fruits and vegetables from our garden without any pesticide, fungicide, insecticide, growth hormones, weedkillers, or any other types of artificial chemical substances are unquestionably much healthier than those from industrial monoculture farms—which account for the majority of products we find in our supermarket.

We don't need to have a garden and can grow our vegetables in our apartment or on the balcony. If you can't grow your vegetables and fruits, you can opt for the produce from regenerative/sustainable farms, which is also positive for all sustainable farmers since, in this way, you also support them.

Not only are the crops you cultivate by yourself good for your health, but the process that you have to go through to take care of them is also good for your health. I have a sedentary lifestyle owing to both my jobs and hobbies and without the garden to take care of, I would never undertake any physical activity at all.

My garden gives me great satisfaction and pleasure. Indeed, it gives me ten times more than it takes—be it something edible like fresh strawberries and vegetables or something inedible, such as bushes and trees with beautiful flowers, leaves, trunks, and twigs.

My garden literally saves me and keeps me healthy both physically and mentally. I don't need to take antidepressants since my mind has never had time to fabricate things or brood over something. Taking care of something alive—especially something so forgiving and grateful like plants and trees—brings me immense joy.

It also gives me a moment of peace and helps me learn to communicate with Nature. Consequently, I do believe that a garden is the best antidepressant, and most importantly, it doesn't have any negative side effects that can wreak havoc on your body and mind.

Chapter 24: Givers, Symbionts, and Parasites

In the kingdom of living things, roughly speaking there are three types of existence: givers who make their existence positive, useful, and helpful to all around them; symbionts who give and take; and parasites that survive by sucking a life force from other life forms.

Givers are undoubtedly the best type of existence but they are a minority, while symbionts are the most common type of existence on the planet, and parasites are, unquestionably, the worst. The parasites are universally harmful that are characterized by greediness and ruthlessness and they are completely egocentric, focusing only on their survival.

Parasites can be plants or animals. Weeds can spread fast and wide, stealing nutrients from other plants as well as suffocating them. It is uncommon for weeds to form a dense carpet or grow taller than other plants, suffocating all around them and stealing light, a food source for plants.

The most common symbionts in the plant world are fungi and trees. Trees absorb carbon in the air and share it with the network of fungi around their roots and fungi feed minerals that plants need. Fungi also allow communication among the trees through their roots. Mother trees can feed their young thanks to the network of fungi around their root. Strong trees can help feed weak trees through the network of fungi. In this way, fungi and trees are in perfect symbiosis.

However, as autotrophs, trees and plants are predominantly givers to all heterotrophs, which is one of the main reasons why I always adore them. Humans are heterotrophs and take the most from Mother Earth and Nature, and till now we (including me) have been parasites to Mother Earth both directly and indirectly: We only take and take from her and many of us are not even grateful and learn to appreciate her.

Actually, humans can be all three of them. We can be parasites to someone like our parents, especially when we are young. All of us are obligate parasites when we are young. However, even when we are obligate parasites, we are still different. Some of us are so needy and hungry, while some ask just a little and others even try to give something back. We can be parasites to the world but givers to some people we love and care for or we can live in symbiosis with most people in society.

Living equates to fighting and struggling. If we choose to live, and we don't want to fight; we will become a burden to all around us because they have to carry us around while fighting their very own wars. I do believe none of us, dignified Homo sapiens, will ever find happiness through that kind of existence.

Even if someone can live without working or doing something useful to society, he/she will never find happiness existing in that way; Homo sapiens intrinsically needs to be fulfilled and satisfied spiritually, which can only mean that we need to find our reasons to live and somehow make our existence useful to others.

While animals and other types of living things do not have much choice because they are dictated to be parasites, symbionts, or givers by birth; humans can choose their types of existence and live their lives harmfully as parasites by exploiting others and sucking them dry, neutrally by giving and taking, or benevolently by giving without expecting anything in return or expecting very little back.

Although we are heavily influenced by our environment, especially our family backgrounds, and our childhood traumas tend to affect us for the rest of our lives or will probably scar us for life; there is still an option for us to choose to let them define us or not.

We can learn from our parents or those who harmed us in our childhood and grow up to become benevolent, opposite to them, or repeat the same mistake and grow up to hurt and harm others. We can live well and happily by making our existence positive and useful to others despite our irresponsible and selfish or mentally ill parents.

We are capable of being born from parasites and mutating ourselves into givers, which makes our species very special. Unlike other living things on Earth, we don't need to be like our parents and we can choose our types of existence. We are not dictated by our genes or family backgrounds. Although we might have a terrible start, it doesn't mean we will have a dramatic ending.

We can be born to parasite parents who thrive by exploiting others but we don't need to grow up to become like them. We can learn from their mistakes and make our existence a blessing to others. Humans can choose and think for themselves, which makes our species unique.

Chapter 25: Love Is all around and Inside of You

When we truly love and care for the plants and trees, they will usually thrive and reward us with all beautiful scents and scenery as well as a healthy environment. The more we love, the more we can perceive love around us and become grateful and feel loved by those around us. The rule of thumb is to feel loved, we need to love others first. If you love all, you will feel loved by all. If you love even the air around you, you will feel loved also by the air.

Life is meaningful only when we learn to love and the more people and things we love, the more positive our existence becomes. When we love, we will spend our time and energy positively and usefully; thus, in the end, our love for others will keep us healthy mentally and physically. Once we exist positively and benevolently, our self-love and self-respect/esteem will be strengthened, and we will also feel loved by ourselves completely.

Our self-respect and self-love will grow each day until it arrives at the point when we will help others only because we want to see them happy or relieve them of their pain and not because we need or want them to love us. This good deed is pure since we don't expect anything in return be it materialistically, emotionally, or spiritually.

Gardening is about loving, giving, nurturing, and caring. It helps us learn how to love and take care of living things. Taking care of plants is stress-free since plants are the least demanding living things on earth as well as the most forgiving.

If you give them the right conditions, such as the right amount of light, fertile soil full of beneficial microorganisms, and humidity; they will thrive and bless you and the environment around you. Even though the conditions you give them are not perfect, they will adapt and thrive on their own. That's how forgiving, grateful, and resilient they are. They teach you how to love and be loved back.

Chapter 26: Defects Are Beautiful

A beautiful garden is not full of plants and trees without defects. Indeed, plants and trees with defects or imperfections can be stunningly beautiful and far more interesting than those impeccable. Broken tulips, for example, are one of the most prized tulips due to their beauty. Broken tulips are, actually, inflicted by a virus, causing them to become variegated and multicolored.

In general, variegation in leaf color occurs because of a lack of green pigment or chlorophyll in some of the plant cells, and in this way, defects give life to real beauties. Genetically speaking, variegation, as well as a virus that gives birth to broken tulips, is a defect, but it results in something flabbergasting, delightful, and captivating.

We can learn from Mother Nature and look at our defects positively. Just like our gardens and plants, our lives, as well as ourselves, are not supposed to be perfect. Defects, traumatic wounds, and all types of pain taken correctly and wisely can make us become amazingly beautiful and wonderfully intriguing.

Some virologists believe that a retrovirus is responsible for the birth of the human race. Without this type of virus, humans would still be chimps. Whether their hypothesis is right or wrong, in any case, defects are common characteristics of life as we know it.

Without defects or problems or challenges, there would be no evolution. The world deprived of challenges is a dead one; as long as there exist lives, measure and countermeasure are bound to be there, and measure without countermeasure spells the end of organisms. Once we choose to exist and live, we have to fight and come up with some countermeasure; otherwise, we won't be able to survive.

We can learn to transform our defects into beautiful things. No matter how painful our past is, we can benefit from it. Our defects make us more interesting, resilient, and unique. Life without problems, pain, and challenges is not life. I have learned to appreciate defects in nature as well as those in me. Only when our hearts embrace own defects can we find peace with ourselves. All of us have defects and wounds, but that doesn't make us less beautiful and lovable.

Chapter 27: Resilience

Plants are incredibly resilient and they will always find a way to survive and spring back to life. Nature is resilient and humans are a part of nature. We have the hidden ability to become resilient if we know how to activate and unlock that power inside us. Whereas plants are resilient by nature, humans need to find the source of their resilience.

To me, the human race is one of the toughest species on Earth. To survive, any life form will have to deal with constant stress and endless challenges physically, mentally, psychologically, and emotionally. All survivors are warriors in one way or another and humans have proved to be one of the strongest warriors on the planet, and the fact that we have survived and thrived until we have overpopulated the planet confirms our success.

The most fundamental element that trickers resilience in humans is love. It might just start from our love for our very own selves and we just want to survive, but that will not be enough in the long run. True and unconditional love for others, instead, is the most powerful stimulus to help us learn to discover our inner strength and recover from any damage done to us. No matter how deep our wound is as long as we learn to love and respect others and ourselves, it will be healed, or at least we can peacefully coexist with it.

Our will to live is the building block of our existence and survival. I do believe that the will to live is intrinsic in all living things. Unlike animals with lower levels of consciousness, however, humans cannot find happiness only to survive physically. As animals with high consciousness, we do have an intrinsic need to survive spiritually.

Accordingly, it is of the utmost importance for humans to make their existence positive for others in one way or another. We need to be convinced that our existence is somehow positive and worth the pain. Love usually gives us the fundamental reason to live and makes us resilient.

Love gives me the strength to get up every morning because I have people and other living things to take care of and to serve. Love strengthens my will to live because I realize that my existence is somehow useful to others—students to teach, friends and family to love and support, Mother Earth to admire and be grateful to, and all people to be kind to.

All in all, love is the most powerful foundation of resilience in humans. Loving only ourselves will never give us enough strength to resist suffering in life. Only when we make our existence useful and helpful to others will we find our purpose in life.

Chapter 28: Garden of Knowledge

I have learned a lot from Nature and I can see the patterns of truth that Mother Nature teaches me through my garden.

To begin with, the garden has taught me that I cannot afford to leave the land empty because all weeds will grow. Since weeds are usually greedy and aggressive, good plants can't compete with them; while empty land without anything growing on it will lead to soil degradation or desertification.

In any case, empty land is not good, so the best way to deal with this situation is to cover the ground with good plants and leave no space for bad plants to grow. There are a lot of good groundcovers and all we need to do is to choose the right plants that will thrive in our gardens and hardiness zone.

This knowledge also makes me think about the way we spend our time and energy. When we have too much time on our hands and don't use it positively, it will wreak havoc both on us and those around us.

According to a body of research, many crimes committed by the young derive from boredom. Those who don't cultivate positive interests are highly likely to spend time doing something negative both toward themselves and others, such as gossiping, watching porn, ruminating about the past, fixating on one's problems, and taking drugs or substances. Please spend your time and energy well and cover your ground with positive activities to prevent weeds to grow in your garden of life.

This concept also makes me think about our political systems. When the country is not governed by a strong and wise government, it will allow evil to take root and cause chaos. Ideally, the government should be wise, knowledgeable, and resourceful. Where there is no benevolent, wise, and strong governor/government; the weeds or the forces of evil will grow and wreak havoc on the country.

As mentioned before, negative organisms are usually stronger and thrive very easily because they focus only on their survival and want to survive at all costs. Due to their nature, unsurprisingly, they are usually greedy and ruthless and will destroy everything in their path. Just like egocentric humans who live their lives focusing only or mostly on their needs, ignoring all others except for themselves.

On the contrary, benevolent and positive people, as well as beneficial organisms, will not only allow others to survive, but will also support others and help them to thrive, and sometimes they even sacrifice their well-being to help others to survive and thrive. Undoubtedly, their lives are much tougher than those of egocentric people/organisms.

While weeds live at the expense of all others and want more and more, keeping most of the surpluses for themselves; beneficial organisms/benevolent humans share their resources with others as well as using them wisely and respectfully. I am trying to learn to live like a benevolent plant, which helps all around it not only to survive but also thrive.

I have learned from nature that for any system to survive, it needs altruism and sacrifices. Egoism, opposite to altruism, will only spell the end of the system. Any system that has too many takers or parasites and not enough givers will come to a tragic end. If we let egoism predominantly guide our lives, humanity, as well as the human race, will eventually die out. Egoism is against life and what is against life is also against us as we are part of living things.

Chapter 29: Phytoremediation

Something that has always amazed me is that although there are a lot of inexpensive, non-toxic, and environmentally friendly solutions; many people opt for expensive, highly toxic, and unsustainable solutions.

All around the world, many lands are abandoned due to chemical contamination and/or other types of pollutants, and if people want to decontaminate them, they will choose to use chemicals to neutralize chemicals, hence synthetic against synthetic.

There are many soil remediation methods: physical/chemical treatment, bioremediation, and thermal, but the most cost-effective and environmentally friendly method, in my opinion, is phytoremediation (classified as bioremediation) by using plants and trees to absorb the pollutants in the soil. Some of them manage to break down the compounds and make them less toxic or non-toxic, while others just store them and isolate the toxin from the environment.

Plants and trees can decontaminate and remove pollutants from the soil by absorbing the pollutants and storing them in their leaves, trunks, roots, or twigs. Sunflowers are known to absorb radiation and were planted in the contaminated lands like Chornobyl, Hiroshima, and Fukushima.

What's more, plants don't only purify the soil, but also the air or their surroundings and they also absorb carbon dioxide, an urgent issue to be solved. Thus, using plants to decontaminate the soil is a win-win-win solution.

That said, the only limitation of phytoremediation is the depth of the tree's root. The trees can decontaminate the soil only as far as their roots can reach. Another issue worth mentioning is it takes some time to purify the environment as plants need time to grow and establish themselves.

Some plants, known as hyperaccumulators, can absorb something much more than others. For example, Alyssum murale can take up to 30,000 micrograms of nickel per one 1 gram dried leaf. However, Alyssum murale is not the only nickel hyperaccumulator; there are a lot of plants that can do the same job. If we learn the properties of plants, we will be able to use the right plants to heal the contaminated sites for us.

Phytoremediation can also be used to increase soil quality. Some soil is not good for growing crops because somehow it has some metal residues and to fix the soil we can use hyperaccumulator plants or they can also be used to intercrop with other food crops. Hyperaccumulators can fix ultramafic soil

Chapter 30: Agromining

gromining is a win-win solution because it can mine the minerals without polluting our environment. However, researchers still need to learn to make it cost-effective and meet the massive demand of the world's increasing hunger for minerals. So far, not all minerals are considered fit for Agromining because the amount of mineral extracted from the plant is too low.

To date, nickel has been one of the most common minerals in Agromining, but I do believe we will also find a cost-effective way to use hyperaccumulators to mine other minerals if researchers have enough funds to support their research.

Another win-win situation would be the use of hyperaccumulators to decontaminate a mining area. Many lands are abandoned after mining and nobody can use them because they are highly toxic. The best solution would be the introduction of the right type of hyperaccumulator plants. In this way, we can harvest minerals and purify the lands at the same time and we can later use the lands for agriculture or other purposes.

Chapter 31: The Garden of My Dream

First and foremost, my dream garden should be able to be completely sustainable and off-grid. It should have its own source of energy and water. To date, my garden has still relied on the water provided by the public utilities. Although I have a solar panel and it reduces the use of gas from the outside source I still rely on gas and electricity provided to us by our government. My dream garden, as well as my dream house, would be completely self-sufficient and autonomous.

I would love to have a big garden since I adore big trees, which are important in the ecosystem because they give shelter as well as food sources to a variety of species. I love a meadow full of wildflowers, but I can't afford to do that due to limited space and I prefer to keep things around my house tidy.

I dream of having a big lake for migratory birds to stop by to take shelter and food. Sadly, I have heard that some people trap and kill migratory birds for food. Killing wildlife for food might be acceptable in the past, but when wild animals have almost been wiped off the face of the earth, it becomes a crime.

Unfortunately, some wild animals are considered to be exquisite traditional dishes, but if I were to choose between human traditions and the equilibrium of our ecosystem, I would definitely choose the latter. When the whole ecosystem completely loses equilibrium, the biosphere will collapse, and humans can't possibly survive.

The garden of my dream would be full of biodiversity and various species as well as sub-species. It would provide shelters, food, and nurseries for wildlife and would be completely free from synthetic substances.

My kitchen garden would follow agroforestry discipline since compared with monoculture, it provides much more food crops and a variety of yields. Moreover, Agroforestry is regenerative and sustainable, while monoculture destroys and poisons the ecosystem. Agroforestry can provide many levels of crop yields. To get the best result from Agroforestry, we also need to know about companion planting. In this way, plants and trees can support each other and thrive together in perfect symbiosis.

We can grow fruit trees and at the lower level some other plants or bushes. I would choose deciduous fruit trees and then something that will need sunlight early in spring and some shelter in summer around the base of the trees. Crop yields in agroforestry are 3 dimensional, while monoculture or conventional farming just gives a one dimensional produce, so it is an ideal way to use the land to its fullest capacity but at the same time it doesn't stress the soil due to companion planting strategy.

Agroforestry and companion planting, however, are not new methods of farming. They were, and still are, used by some smallholder farmers. The Three Sisters, for example, is one of the companion planting techniques that has existed for a long time. Originally, this planting technique was used by Native Americans. Corn, bean, and squash are planted together because they nurture each other just like sisters who love and support each other.

Beans, like almost all legumes, fertilize the soil with nitrogen, from which corn and squash can benefit. In return, beans are supported by the corn stalks because they need something to wind around, and the squash leaves provide ground cover between corns and beans and prevent weeds to grow. All these three types of plants thrive much better together than being planted alone.

Actually, Mother Earth is my dream garden. Without our destruction, she would be something similar to the Garden of Eden. We are just her guests and we must respect our Host. Humans do not own the planet. We equally share the earth with other living things on the planet. We are not a master of the planet and can do whatever we see fit. Mother Earth is not our slave or something to control and exploit—if anything, the Earth is our mother. Without her, our mother, grandmother, great-grandmother, great-great-grandmother, and so on could never exist or survive.

Chapter 32: A Garden Junkie

I think at this point you have already guessed that I am addicted to gardening and Nature and I would happily accept that. I really am a full-blown nature/garden junkie. There are differences between addiction to drugs and Nature though.

To begin with, while drugs destroy both our physical and mental health, Nature heals us and keeps us healthy both mentally and physically.

Second, the effects of drugs wear off, while the excitement of nature junkies never fades away. Every time I visit my garden, there are always things to do and even more things to admire. I smile when I am in the garden and remain in a good mood even much later, so I am practically permanently high!!!

Third, a garden makes you hopeful, whereas drugs make you become or remain hopeless. All garden junkies look forward to seeing all flowers bloom in their seasons, and when the flowers fade, we will hope to see them again next year.

Fourth, nature junkies will try to save the environment in one way or another, whereas drugs might make those who are addicted to them lose interest in life altogether.

Fifth, nature junkies are usually active and productive. The beauty of nature keeps them alert, enthusiastic, and wide awake; while drugs make people completely lose touch with reality.

Sixth, garden junkies never feel depressed or lonely because they learn to communicate with Nature and She becomes their best friend, which allows nature junkies to find happiness when they are alone and they never need to seek company. However, as they are peaceful and pleasant, many people like them, so they are hardly left alone.

Seventh, satisfaction is fundamental for Homo sapiens since, unlike other species, we need to fulfill our spiritual needs. Like it or not, humans need to feel satisfied with their existence, and gardening gives satisfaction as plants and trees are not needy, are so forgiving and resilient, and reward you much more than what you give to them. Givers are normally grateful and when someone gives something to them, they will give back 10 times more than what they receive. If you love and take care of nature, satisfaction is guaranteed.

In conclusion, if you must be addicted to something, please choose to be a Nature junkie; and I promise you will be more positive, relaxed, peaceful, healthy, loveable, joyful, hopeful, and happy.

Chapter 33: All-encompassing Love

A beautiful garden should be full of various colors and textures, and we also need plants with diverse types of resistance to disease and/or extreme environments to guarantee that our garden will remain beautiful all year round under different conditions and types of weather.

Just like a garden, the world could become a beautiful place if we learn to embrace people who are different from us as well as all other life forms on our planet. We need all professions, skills, talents, and viewpoints to find equilibrium and help us survive and contribute to our progress—the differences should not separate but unite us.

We should try to listen to different opinions and viewpoints and learn to look at things from their standpoints and angles. All kinds of skills, intelligence, talents, and knowledge can be used positively or negatively. All we need to do is to learn to use them skillfully and benevolently guided by All-encompassing Love and not selective love or egocentrism. We can also help each other by encouraging those around us to use their skills positively to find their place in the world we all share.

Even when we find those with twisted minds who use their abilities egocentrically and hurt others, we shouldn't hate them as hate is negative both for ourselves and others. Under no circumstances is hate positive and even though it has a negative effect on both those who hate and those who are the targets of hate, the most negative impact will be on those who hate.

All unskillful and negative deeds are the fruits of wrong attitudes. Listening to them can help us see the world from different angles as well as helping us to learn to forgive them. Although none of their negative deeds are justifiable, we should at least try to understand them.

There are both positive and negative sides of life/nature. Some take part in the negative side, some are both negative and positive, while others are predominantly positive. To me, the worst nightmare would be being condemned to be born not to suffer myself but to make others suffer. If it totally depended on me, I would always choose to love universally and be on the positive side of the universe.

However, from what I could see most evil people have their causes and hardly any of them are born evil. In any case, we should never treat them cruelly. Abusing and maltreating those we believe to be bad/evil will transform us into evil ourselves. Evil is not the cause of itself but the consequence of ignorance/wrong attitudes/ negative mindsets or sets of values—most of which have been indoctrinated into us since we were young.

Those who live their lives guided by greed and egoism have their cause(s). Family backgrounds are one of the most influential causes. They might not be taught, especially by example, to learn to love and respect others. They are brought up to take things for granted instead of living with gratitude. Most of us are heavily influenced by our families and our childhood usually has a great impact on us even we become adults.

Whatever pain we have been through, it's never too late to improve ourselves as long as we learn to love and respect others and ourselves. We can learn to transform our pain into something beautiful like broken tulips or variegated plants.

A garden or Nature makes us understand the value and the power of peace. To find true inner peace, however, we should cultivate forgiveness and then let all our painful past go. In this way, we can find peace with ourselves and others. Once we find inner peace, we will automatically live in harmony with others as well as ourselves.

A garden, as well as our lives, thrives only when it finds harmony. Our peaceful coexistence is impossible unless we learn to love, respect, and forgive each other. The best type of love that will have a large-scale impact on the world is All-encompassing Love since it includes all others and not only a selective and limited group of people or living things. Mother Earth allows all living things to thrive on her and loves universally, and we can learn from her and love like her.

Let Mother Nature heal you, allow Mother Earth to nourish you, and let your garden give you hope.